A Priest's Journal of Hope

A Priest's Journal of Hope

◆

–God and 9/11–

By Philip C. Linder

iUniverse, Inc.
New York Lincoln Shanghai

A Priest's Journal of Hope
–God and 9/11–

iUniverse, Inc.

For information address:
iUniverse, Inc.
2021 Pine Lake Road, Suite 100
Lincoln, NE 68512
www.iuniverse.com

Cover Design by Colleen Coletta; Art work used in design by Philip C. Linder.

ISBN: 0-595-30413-3

Printed in the United States of America

Dedicated to Ellen, my love and partner on the journey and to all who search for the peace of God.

Contents

INTRODUCTION

I walked the coast of a South Carolina beach in the sixteenth year of my priesthood questioning my faith, and even more, wondering who was this God of September 11th? This problem was, of course, not uniquely mine, but one with which I had to wrestle personally if I was to continue on my spiritual journey.

The journey I was on officially began several thousand feet above the U.S.S. Coral Sea in the summer of 1979. I was a midshipman in the United States Naval Reserve on my first summer of active duty, flying in a rescue chopper during flight operations over the Pacific Ocean. When one is strapped to the deck of a maneuvering helicopter over a vast ocean for five hours, there is a lot of time to think. For me, it was the beginning of actually listening—listening to the steady voice of God that had for many years been calling me into relationship. When the chopper finally landed on that aircraft carrier, I had unknowingly landed, as well, at the genesis of what would become a lifelong journey.

Ever since that day, the ocean has called me back over and over again—only God could have created such a magnificent thing. I dip my fingers in the sea and taste its salt, and I taste God. The ebb and flow of the ocean has a way of reminding us of a God that sometimes seems like a high tide right upon us, and at other times seems as low as the tide that withdraws from our reach.

Just like the tide that comes in and goes out, there is an ebb and flow to our spiritual life. At times God is right upon us, and at other times God seems quite withdrawn, if not totally absent. Within the spiritual life we are reminded that both are necessary movements if our faith is to deepen. Every day the tide comes in and goes out—like it or not. The tide can serve as a constant reminder that—like it or not—God will seem both closer and more distant at different times in our lives.

I had always believed that the key to the spiritual journey was to live faithfully within whatever tide you found yourself walking. As I walked the beach at high tide for the first time following September 11th, it became painfully evident that the faith that I had known, as well as the God who had called me, was in that ocean under my feet in a different way. The question that confronts us is whether or not we are willing to engage the spiritual life in a meaningful way, even in the most difficult times? Are we willing to seek God—to be all God desires for us?

Philip C. Linder
Easter 2003—on the coast of South Carolina

FINDING GOD

Reflections before 9-11

PURCHASE BEWILDERMENT

Well, there I was, in total darkness without even a hint of moonlight. It is so beautiful to be out in the darkness of the woods waiting for the sun to come up. In the silent darkness you can sense God's presence. As sunrise approaches, it is amazing how many sounds begin to emerge all around you. At one point I heard something that was very close and very foreign sounding—*shooshooshooshooshshoosh!* I thought…*what was that? A snake*? It was one of those rare moments. Certainly I have had the experience of swimming in the ocean and feeling something brush up alongside of me. On the coast of South Carolina that is quite significant, as we have jellyfish the size of small basketballs. What is interesting about adults when something underwater brushes us is that we pretend we are not worried at all—we freeze and quietly lift our knees toward our chest and pray that it will go away. What I love about children is that when they feel something creepy up against them they scream and flap about—there is no mistaking that they have just been brushed! Maybe they have the right idea; it has been said by the great teachers that perhaps we should sell our cleverness and purchase bewilderment.

"All of them were filled with the Holy Spirit and began to speak in other languages, as the Sprit gave them ability…And at this sound the crowd gathered and was bewildered, because each one heard them speaking in the native language of each." (Acts 2:3, 5) The birth of the Christian Church may have seemed as apparent confusion to the clever. What could possibly have been happening in that great gathering on the day the church was born? Could the person who thought of him or her as being 'oh so clever' have ever figured it out?

I walk into the midst of that great gathering over 2000 years ago and hear all of the confusion of many languages being spoken at the same time. Imagining the sounds…imagining the sights. What is my state of mind? Is my approach one of bewilderment, or is it one of cleverness? And how do I approach my faith in God? The birth of the church was at the same time the birth of an approach to God—an approach of bewilderment. The scope of the languages being spoken amazed and astonished the crowd; the power of God was in their midst and invited them to bewilderment—bewilderment before God. And through their bewilderment they came to hear and understand the language of God that spoke to each of them.

William James stated, "Our belief at the beginning of a doubtful undertaking is the one thing that ensures the successful outcome of our venture." Bewilderment before God allowed the first Christians to move beyond the noise and confusion to hear God's voice and see a vision for the future. And it is this kind of openness, this kind of imaginative questioning, and this kind of bewilderment before God that empowers you to be all that God would have you be. Michelangelo once said, "The greater danger for most of us is not that our aim is too high and we miss it, but that it is too low and we reach it."

So what is your approach to God? Are you willing to embrace bewilderment before the power and possibilities of God? How high is your aim in life? For when you approach God with bewilderment, you acknowledge God's power and possibilities for your life. With the power of the Holy Spirit you can set high aims for the life you lead. Then let us sell our cleverness and purchase bewilderment. Let us live and aim high in the power of God's Spirit.

PRESENTATION

The sun would be going down and the air chilling rapidly, as we sat in pews facing one another for the close of the day. The hour was 5:30 p.m. when the community of faith in Chelsea Square gathered to sing Evensong in the Chapel of the Good Shepherd. As each day and each year passed at The General Theological Seminary, it was *The Song of Simeon—Nunc dimittis,* that pushed my walk in faith forward: "Lord, now lettest thou thy servant depart in peace, according to thy word; For mine eyes have seen thy salvation, which thou hast prepared before the face of all people, to be a light to enlighten the Gentiles, and to be the glory of thy people Israel." (Luke 2:29-32)

I cannot say enough of the comfort and strength that those words from the second chapter of Luke's gospel brought to me. They were ever-powerful reminders that like Simeon, when we meet Christ face to face, we can move forward in our faith journeys...in our daily lives...with strength and the peace of God, no matter what our present situation.

These words of Simeon are spoken some 40 days after the birth of Jesus. Jesus, according to Jewish practice, is presented or dedicated to God in the Temple. Simeon, a faithful observer of the Jewish faith, is waiting in the Temple to meet Christ. And when he sees him in Mary's arms, Simeon acknowledges Jesus as Lord and Messiah. Simeon proclaims Christ to be a light to reveal God to all the nations—to be the glory of the nation of Israel. Simeon's words were so powerful that even Mary and Joseph were amazed. The prophet Anna, in her great age and wisdom, witnesses the Song of Simeon, and not only confirms his words, but speaks as well of this child as the one who is to bring redemption.

Jesus, even as he is still an infant in his mother's arms, is understood as having significance for all people. So what is your experience of meeting Christ? Has he presented himself to you? What is the significance of seeing Him in your life?

The stained glass windows of the cathedral in which I serve are incredibly beautiful. Yet, there is one that captured my spirit and love from the very first. The window, located in the Baptistry, is a 1910 German rendering of *The Presentation of Jesus in the Temple*. It depicts Joseph holding a pair of turtledoves; Mary, the mother of Jesus at his side; Simeon holding the Christ child; and Anna in the shadows. So where has Christ presented himself to you? Can you say, "I have seen him; I can now go forward in peace…I can persevere no matter what my situation."

THE WAITING ROOM

Every day of our lives there is some time spent waiting. Perhaps we wait for the alarm clock to sound a new day. We wait for the breakfast toast to pop up. We wait at the first red light we encounter. We wait for phone calls, facsimiles, and e-mails. We wait in line to pay for the groceries, purchase new items at the department store, or to be seated in a restaurant. We even wait at times to be waited on. But some of the most serious waiting we do in life is found in those times that we are in a hospital waiting room, waiting for the news from the doctor of how a loved one is doing.

My wife and I found ourselves in such a waiting room. Hours earlier we received that dreaded phone call that all parents fear—that their child had been involved in an accident. Our youngest son was one of the passengers in a friend's car that was in a head on collision with a drunk driver of another vehicle. At 6:00 p.m. we were in the waiting room of the triage center of an emergency room, waiting to hear that our son did not sustain any serious head injuries. There we met others who were in that place, and silently shared a bond through the thoughts and emotions that ran through our minds and hearts. As a priest, I have many times been in hospital waiting rooms with church members; however, this time my priesthood was overshadowed by my parenthood, and I yearned for the God I can usually so easily rely on for others.

Waiting rooms, those uncomfortable places of hard worn furniture with tired bodies and fast food trash, are icons of our longings for God in the barren times of life. The Psalmist cried out that we are, "in a barren and dry land where there is no water." (Psalm 63) Where is God as we sit and make idle chatter? Where is God in our pacing upon the worn carpet? God is in that waiting room.

We experience God in waiting because it is then that we become fully aware of how little we are in control. Although I firmly believe that God does not cause the pain and suffering that we experience, I know that God is found there. God is in the waiting room sitting, pacing, embracing, and drying our eyes, "Yea though I walk through the valley of the shadow of death, I will fear no evil; for thou art with me; thy rod and the thy staff, they comfort me." (Psalm 23)

It wasn't easy encountering God that night in the waiting room. However, in my yearning for Him, God was revealed in the others in that waiting room—family, friends, doctors, nurses, and the priest who came to be at his side. God is in the waiting room, and the spiritual journey is one where you at times find yourself waiting for God, and at other times God waiting for you and on you.

GOD AND UNDERSTANDING

Driving back to the cathedral after a most difficult hospital visit, I was not only stopped at a red light, I was stopped as well in my faith. I stared through the front windshield of my car with the profound realization that I did not understand God at all. This was a moment of crisis in faith for me—how was I to bring others to an understanding of God if I could not claim it for myself?

This life that we live has the potential to impose real difficulties and hardships upon us. Theologically I know that this is because we have our being in a fallen and imperfect world—we do not live in the Garden of Eden. I also believe with every ounce of my being that God sent His Son Jesus Christ into the world to redeem us from this sin and imperfection—that when these bad things happen we have access to God through the forgiveness and eternal life that Christ died for on the cross. I know all these things, yet I do not understand God.

I returned to my office and reached not for my Book of Common Prayer, but rather the dictionary. Webster's Dictionary defines understanding as: *a mental grasp, or comprehension.* I was humbled as I read those words and thought how could I ever claim to have a mental grasp of God? What I do have is faith in God, and faith in God is very different than understanding God and all of God's ways. You see, understanding through faith takes on a whole new dimension and meaning.

Jesus said, "Peace is what I leave with you; it is my own peace that I give you. I do not give it as the world does. Do not be worried and upset; do not be afraid." (John 14:27) And it is St. Paul who ties this peace to understanding with his words: "and the peace of God, which surpasses all understanding, will guard your hearts and minds in Christ Jesus." (Philippians 4:7)

These words tell you God's peace is greater than any of our attempts at understanding in the midst of life's difficult situations and conditions. And it is your faith and hope in that peace of God that makes it ok not to understand as the world so often requires.

So the light turns green and you begin to move forward. The road you travel is not necessarily an easy one; however, it is made livable through God's peace, through the blessing prayer you hear pronounced as you leave church on Sunday—*The peace of God which passes all understanding keep your hearts and minds in the knowledge and love of God, And of His Son Jesus Christ our Lord.*

WHAT IS YOUR SOIL TYPE

I am trying to remember the last time that I was caught in a sudden rainstorm. I mean one of those times that there was no escaping it; I was going to get wet. And I don't mean just a little wet—I mean soaked!

A number of years ago, while living in Atlanta, I went to the Atlanta Zoo for a photography class that I was taking. The day was one of the hottest I had ever experienced. Of course, that was prior to moving to Columbia, South Carolina. The animals were very lethargic, and I hadn't yet caught on film that magical moment I had hoped to bring back to the class for a grade. I was really hot and exhausted as late afternoon and an impending thunderstorm approached. As I sat on a bench near the park's entrance and unloaded my camera it happened. The clouds burst open and it rained as hard as I have ever witnessed. And at just that moment, a group of elementary school children came thundering around the bend, laughing and soaked in their bright colored clothing, as they headed for the bus. The magical photographic moment had arrived and my camera was empty. We were all drenched from the rain, and I was out of film. Rule number one of our instructor had been, "Always be prepared to respond."

Jesus said, "A sower went out to sow. And as he sowed, some seeds fell on the path, and the birds came and ate them up. Others fell on rocky ground, where they did not have much soil…and since they had no root they withered away. Other seed fell among thorns, and the thorns grew up and choked them. Other seeds fell on good soil and brought forth grain…" (Matthew 13:3-8)

There is a test that I presently administer to couples as part of their pre-marriage work called the Meyers-Briggs Personality Test. A number of sophisticated studies have shown that knowing your partner's *type*, or way of interpreting and responding to life's situations, can be an important key to a flourishing and lasting relationship. Indeed, Meyers-Briggs is a helpful test in the understanding of ourselves, and this in turn gives us insight into all of our relationships. I have taken the test four times and each time I clearly test as an ENFJ—an extroverted, intuitive, feeling, judging personality type. Of course, for this to make sense we have to study the definition of those terms. My pressing question, though, is not what is my personality type, but rather, what is my soil type?

If Jesus intended for us to understand the sower to be God, and I believe that he did, we have before us an amazing image of God indiscriminately throwing seed in all directions. The Word of God, the teachings of Jesus Christ—handfuls of them—being thrown everywhere onto all kinds of soils. Can you see it? Isn't it just like the heavy rain from the heavens that drenches everyone equally? It does not discriminate.

As Jesus proclaimed God's Word, it was his hearers' vision of reality that affected whether or not his teaching took root. Their vision of reality determined their soil type, and so it is with you today. Does your vision of reality embrace sin—dishonesty, abusive behaviors, hurtful words and practices toward others? Does your vision of reality include a strong character, especially under trial? Does your vision of reality inappropriately embrace the things of the world? What is your soil type?

A sad and vivid example of bad soil types has been all over the evening news recently. We have lost a great deal of confidence in corporate America because some corporations and their chief executive officers have acted out of a vision of reality that has no depth. Shallow corporate greed and untruthfulness embraced a vision of reality that is the antithesis of the life to which God invites all. Likewise in Christ's day, there were visions of reality that would not let God's Word take hold—take root. Yet then, like today, God scattered his loving Word everywhere. When God's Word falls on you does it take root and flourish?

What Jesus is inviting us to is a life that places Him as the master of our reality. It is both a lifelong invitation and one to which we must continually R.S.V.P. "Yes, Lord, I am going to hear your Word of truth and it will direct my heart, mind, body and soul." When my oldest son was only three, he loved to help me in our yard work. He used to follow right behind me with his little plastic lawnmower as I cut the grass. Yet, what I remember most is the time he walked alongside me reaching his hand into the bucket of grass seed indiscriminately throwing it all about with me at planting time. I think that is what God ultimately invites you to do. To be good soil…be prepared to respond…flourish in God's work…and walk alongside God, joining in the scattering of His seed.

THE WHISTLE OF GOD

I still remember as a little boy stopping in my tracks to hear the train whistle sounding. The air had to be clear and the wind blowing in the right direction for the sound to travel to our yard from about a mile away. Yet, when that right combination came together, boy could you hear that whistle.

Just recently, at 3:00 a.m., I was awakened on the street on which I now live to that whistle again. I thought about the house I grew up in; I could picture that train following along on the tracks and reflected upon how that whistle can wake us up at any time. The train passed and I wondered whether God whistled at times to get my attention as well.

It would seem that there are different hours or times when we hear the whistle of God announcing He is about to do a new thing in our lives. We may remember back to some significant religious experience or event, and recall that somehow then God seemed to be getting our attention in a new and clear way. Could God have been whistling? Webster's Dictionary defines whistling as: *to produce a clear sharp sound; to summon, or signal.*

When I was twenty and a junior in college, a constant sound echoed in the back of all of my thoughts and actions. For months I searched and prayed over what that sound was all about.

Looking back, it was like the whistle of God preparing His coming into my life in a new and bold way that ultimately changed my vocation. God was, of course, calling me to the priesthood. You see, God's whistle comes to each of us at all hours and different times, summoning us to serve and calling us to new life in God. Like that 3:00 a.m. train whistle, maybe this also was a time when God was seeking to wake me up to what God would have my life be about. Perhaps this is the hour when you will hear the whistle of God in a way that will stop you in your tracks.

SAY YES

The voice of one crying out in the wilderness is that of John the Baptist, who emerges to announce the coming of the Messiah. John appeared clothed in camel's hair to preach that there was One coming: "who is mightier than I, the thong of whose sandals I am not worthy to stoop down and untie." (Mark 1:7) John baptized with water, but he would baptize with the Holy Spirit. John was proclaiming *kairos*, a time when all flesh would see the salvation of God.

"Prepare the way of the Lord, make his paths straight." (Mark 1:3) John's was a baptism of repentance; it was a call for the preparation of one's heart, mind and soul for the coming of Christ, so that the saving grace of God in Jesus might reach everyone. Although God's grace does not depend on our doing or thinking anything, still there is an appropriate act of faith, of preparation on the individual's part. There is our capacity for reformation, for opening our hearts to the ways and will of God. It is God who acts...God who saves...God who redeems, yet God looks to us to say a resounding YES to His divine initiative in our lives.

When you say yes to God, you strike up a powerful partnership with God whereby you can expect the best for your life and actually get it. This does not mean that you will receive everything you think you want, but rather that your yes to God's initiatives in your life will put you in harmony with God's will. Preparing the way of the Lord is opening yourself up to God in ways that strengthen your faith, and will make that which has seemed impossible for you a real possibility. What needs to happen in your spiritual life? Preparing the way of the Lord is learning to believe. Can you hear the Baptist's words to: "Prepare the way of the Lord, make his paths straight", as a call to partnership with God, to saying yes to God's initiatives in your life?

PURPLE PONDERING

There is a secret I have. Every time that I go to the beach—one of the great joys of my life—I go down to the ocean soon after my arrival to take a walk by myself. And at some point on that walk, I bend down and dip my fingers in the ocean and then place them on my lips to taste the saltiness. Yet for me, it is not about tasting the salt, it is instead really about tasting God. I am certain that God, the very essence of God, is in that ocean. I know that I am close to him on that walk along the shore.

I am not entirely certain about why I go through that ritual, but I think that it has something to do with a burning desire to have God fill my life. And so the question arises, why do I need to have such a burning desire?

Shortly after his resurrection, Christ appears to the disciples on the road to Emmaus—that wonderful story that many artists throughout the centuries have beautifully portrayed. The disciples do not recognize Jesus, and they explain to him at length all of the things that had just happened in their lives and to their Lord. However, when they invite this stranger to stay and have supper with them we read: "When he was at table with them, he took bread, blessed and broke it, and gave it to them. Then their eyes were opened, and they recognized him; and he vanished from their sight. They said to each other, 'Were not our hearts burning within us?'" (Luke 24:29-32) What burns within you? What is the burning desire of your life?

Perhaps Advent, one of the most sacred seasons of the church year, can be a time when you look out amongst the red, green and white lights and ponder instead in purple. Advent, derived from the Latin word *Adventus,* means coming—the coming of the Lord. Early Christians in the western tradition understood these days before Christmas in two different ways: some as a time of repentance and others as time of joyous celebration. And it seems that we live in the midst of that tension to this day, yet I believe that preparation is inherent throughout.

Advent is especially a time of the preparation of our souls for God's Son. It is again our walk toward the celebration of the birth of the One who calls us into a life of faith and commitment. These are days to look beyond the many colors of the season and ponder instead in purple—a color that symbolizes both repentance and preparation. This is a time to wait upon God in a way that you never have before, in a way that suggests God to be the burning desire of your life. It is, if you will, a time of moving toward full incarnation—toward becoming more of what you are already—a child of God.

What is your heart's burning desire? Why not ponder in purple? Perhaps you will find the answer to be a deeper knowing of God.

SNOWING DOWN

On a Monday afternoon, at three o'clock, I stopped with my son at the local grocery store just in case the weather worsened. At the time it was raining heavily and the store was reasonably empty. We started making the rounds for milk, orange juice, bread and eggs, when my son exclaimed, "Hey Dad, look! It's snowing!" Sure enough it was. And by the time we turned the corner of the last aisle, the checkout lines were eight people deep. Needless to say, I was pleased that Monday was my day off, and that we had gotten an early start and were headed home.

I hadn't seen a snowfall like that in a number of years. As we were driving home, I could tell from my years of living in snow country that this was a snow that was going to stick. Several hours later, there was a beautiful white blanket across the city and things seemed very different.

There is something about a fresh snowfall that changes time and space. A neighbor stopped over and told us that we needed to come outside and play in the snow, so we did. We walked down our street with the children, and greeted lots of folks walking with children and dogs. Everyone seemed happier and more willing to look each other in the eyes and greet one another. In between seeing folks, I noticed how quiet it seemed, and how absolutely beautiful everything looked.

Snowing down is what I think best describes what happens with a new snowfall. People slow down from the hectic pace of life, appreciate the beauty of God's creation, and more readily notice and greet one another. Perhaps snow is one more way that God creates sacred time and space. Church architects discovered early on that stained glass windows in churches and cathedrals were one way of creating sacred time and space—a place set apart for prayer and reflection, without daily and worldly distractions. I think in a unique way snowfalls perform the very same task.

When you find yourself in a new snow, do you slow down? What are the ways that you create your own snowfalls—set apart time and space to talk to God and reflect on that relationship? You know, there really is something about a new snowfall that changes everything.

A TIME IN THE WILDERNESS

Several Christmases ago I heard for the first time a beautiful song written by Carole Bayer Sager and David Foster entitled, *The Prayer*. This past year I was reminded of it again. The words go something like this, "I pray you'll be our eyes and watch us where we go. And help us to be wise in times when we don't know. Let this be our prayer as we go our way. Lead us to a place. Guide us with your grace; to a place where we'll be safe."

The spiritual journey is one that centers upon the notion of our lives...of our faith...as being led by a power that is greater than us and at times beyond our understanding. "Jesus was led up by the Spirit into the wilderness—for forty days and forty nights." (Mark: 12-13) Today, am I open to being led by the Spirit of God into the wilderness?

Wilderness places and experiences by their very nature embody uncertainty and disorder, if not a sense of chaos. We know that after Jesus was baptized and God proclaimed him from the heavens to be his beloved Son with whom he was well pleased, Christ did not head out to a baptism party—he went instead to a place of uncertainty...a place of chaos...a place of hunger...and a place of temptation. Jesus went for a time in the wilderness.

Are you presently in the wilderness because of a difficult circumstance—an illness, a loss, a death—that has been thrust upon you? Have you been catapulted into the wilderness because of the power of sin that you have let take over in your life? Or, do you need to choose to enter the wilderness to grow in your life in God? Might you willingly face uncertainty, chaos, hunger and temptation? And, do you trust that God will always lead you with His grace, to a place where you will grow in faith and be safe?

ALL MY LIFE

There is constant amazement in the ways that God speaks to us through other people in what are sometimes the most difficult of situations. The steady voice of God interrupts the silence and awkwardness of a conversation that struggles because of the moment.

I remember that cold sunny day that I headed to the funeral home to be present for a family during their time of loss. This was the family of a deceased person that I had never met, and I knew little of the family. He had died of natural causes well into his eighties, and as I arrived I pondered the words and presence that I could offer.

After greetings, condolences, and plans were arranged for the service, I asked his wife: "How long have you and your husband been married?" I expected her to give me the number of years. Instead, she paused, a tear ran down her cheek and she responded, "All my life." All of us in the room welled up with tears. I took her hand and knew that she had spoken from deep within her heart, and that God had spoken through her as well from that same place.

A relationship of love that has no memory of beginning, but rather just being and enduring, is what God hopes for from us. Perhaps at our own death God will ask us, "How long have you known me?" Will our response be, "All my life?" I believe that God desires such an answer. Can you strive to live this way—in this knowing? What are the implications of this kind of relationship with God?

You see, to know God is a very different thing than simply believing in Him. To believe something is not the same as to know something. One may believe that they can swim because they have studied others swimming and read books on the subject; however, until one gets in the water and flounders around one cannot know swimming. The same is true with your relationship with God. To know God embodies belief, but beyond that it requires a daily life lived intentionally with God at the center of all that you say, all that you do and all that you think.

Imagine Christ asking you, "How long have you known me?" Imagine responding, "All my life." Imagine living your life today in a way that brings forth such an answer to God.

EXPERIENCING GOD IN WAR AND PEACE

Reflections following 9-11

PRAYER, TRUST AND COURAGE

The horrific terrorist acts perpetrated on Tuesday, September 11th brought us as a people of faith to a place that most of us have never experienced or even imagined. What initially seemed to be a tragic accident was soon revealed as an act of evil, the magnitude of which most of us never believed could be possible on the shores of our nation. It was one of those days that we will always remember—like Pearl Harbor and the assassinations of President Kennedy and Dr. Martin Luther King, Jr. For what these days have in common is the apparent victory of evil over good, and the haunting question of where God is at this time?

Wherever we physically found ourselves the day those four planes were fatally hijacked, the World Trade Center collapsed and the Pentagon was attacked, we all emotionally found ourselves struggling to understand how something like this could happen. I found myself asking factual type questions: *Who could do such an evil thing? How could our national intelligence and security fail us so greatly? How many people were injured, or died? What does this mean for us?* I was glued to my television seeking answers. Finally, overwhelmed, I fell to my knees.

This was a time to pray. The evil that was carried out against our nation and humanity was unparalleled in modern history. Evil is something we are often uncomfortable speaking of and prefer to pretend does not exist. Yet the manifestation of evil through these terrorist acts makes it impossible for any one of us to deny its reality. Evil is real. Evil is that which is not of God, and what makes it all the more insidious is when it is masked within the guise of a religion. There is not one of the credible world religions, including Islam, which teaches the murder of innocent people. And it is the very reality of the evil of these terrorist acts that calls people of every faith to pray.

I believe with all that I am that God is present with us at all times, and especially in the tragic times of darkness and despair. The words of the 23rd Psalm ring out like the bells of a cathedral: "Yea, though I walk through the valley of the shadow of death, I shall fear no evil, for thou art with me." You must ask God for the kind of trust needed for these words to have power in my life.

Perhaps above all else, you must pray to God for courage to meet days and challenges that are evil. Evil is real. God's goodness, however, will never succumb to it. God does not let us down. Rather, God stands with us and gives us courage to look evil straight in the eyes and with his wisdom and grace respond. The baptismal service in the Episcopal Church asks: "Do you renounce the evil powers of this world which corrupt and destroy the creatures of God?" Do you have the courage to proclaim a resounding yes?

STEPPING BEYOND THE CHECKPOINT

Unexpected emotions from time to time can take us totally by surprise. Traveling for the first time following the tragic day of September 11th, I was not at all apprehensive about flying. I do not fear my own death, just the ramifications for my family and church. So, when I became deeply saddened as I moved beyond the checkpoint, I was stunned.

Stepping beyond the checkpoint, I suddenly realized that life in America had changed dramatically. Of course, I had already believed that, but now, I was coming to know it. The sight of armed National Guardsmen in the airport was also a vision of a nation where this was now normative. We had lost an innocence that was long ago shattered in most of the rest of the world.

Later, during the flight, I realized that in a unique way my faith paralleled that very experience. The spiritual journey invites me to step beyond the checkpoint. That checkpoint is a bit different for each of us. However, its essence is the same—it is the place where we stop just short of living our life fully for God. So, the question to consider is, *where is my checkpoint?*

The checkpoint is the place where you can consciously choose to move from being a believer in God to knowing God. This transformation occurs through the daily choices and practices of your life. What choices and practices of living keep you from moving past the checkpoint?

Within the life of faith, the checkpoint is a place of your own checking and of God's checking of you. It is the place where you examine the choices and practices that keep you from knowing God. However, it is also the place where God may direct you to give up, take on, or change—and that can be uncomfortable.

As I returned home, I was stopped at the checkpoint to have my carry-on bag searched, and then was asked to remove my shoes. I really was not looking forward to doing either, but checkpoints are like that sometimes.

So are you willing to step beyond the checkpoint? Are you willing to have your bags searched and take off your shoes? Are you willing to consciously choose to move from believing in God to knowing God?

APPROACHING SEPTEMBER 11th

As the anniversary of September 11th approaches, there seems to be a natural resurgence among many of similar emotions and thoughts expressed on that fateful day. There is the natural anxiousness of the very anniversary of that date that brings fears of another terrorist attack. There is also still evident a profound sadness and mourning for the lives that were lost that day, as well as an innocence that we as a people shall no longer be able to claim. We will never again be naïve to the possible evil threats of terrorism. Perhaps more than anything else, though, we know deep within our hearts that this day will now for evermore be different. We cannot simply go about business as usual on that day.

How can we as people of God approach September 11th? Maybe the place that we will naturally want to begin is by remembering all of those who without preparation were called upon to give their lives. We must never lose sight of the cold fact that within four hijacked planes, the World Trade Center, the Pentagon and one field in Pennsylvania, some three thousand men, women and children lost their lives. We can never forget that fact, nor forget that these were not numbers but real people, innocent civilians striving to faithfully live their lives. Five-year-old Molly, who lost her dad in the Twin Towers, was told by her mom that God had pulled her daddy up to heaven from the devastation. Her question back to her mother was "Does God have enough hands?" Certainly God does and so do we. Each September 11th we must always stop from the business of the day to put our hands together to God and remember all who lost their lives and all who were left behind to mourn their deaths.

However, September 11th also calls us to envision a horizon that we are yet unable to see because of all the clouds. These are the clouds of hatred. These are the clouds of hatred caused by diversity, the very diversity that God has given to his creation as a gift. These are the clouds of hatred caused by a world that is often unwilling to seek solutions to the issues of poverty and injustice. These are clouds that on September 11th we pray may one day be lifted, so that we see clearly a horizon where all of God's people may live in peace. This is a horizon that we must not only pray for, but believe in, for on a round planet there is ultimately no choosing up sides.

In the final analysis, September 11th will never again be a day of normal business. May you seek ways to approach this day that combines a collective remembering of those who suffered and died, along with prayers for a world where all may one day live in peace.

QUESTIONS IN AUTUMNAL TIMES

It happens every year, yet this year it was so much more pronounced. The leaves changed to vibrant colors of red, yellow and orange; and as they began to fall so my spirit did as well. As the days got shorter and the air began to chill, I felt a bit melancholic—fall has a way of encouraging this experience. The tragic fall of 2001, though, had reminded me ever so poignantly that life is always changing and uncertain. And this autumn, I have many more questions than in the autumns of years past.

Each of us processed the events of September 11th in our own unique way. Yet, I believe that at some level we have all grappled with how uncertain and vulnerable our lives now seem. What has been most disheartening to me, though, is the pervasive sense of hurt throughout the world. Questions that emerge center around how humanity could perpetrate such violence and hatred—how people could conceive and execute plans of using commercial planes as missiles and sending Anthrax through the mail? In a more general sense we have had to confront the sad realities of human behavior. Put most simply, how can people be so incredibly hurtful toward one another? These are questions that have quite frankly kept me awake in the middle of many fall nights.

We can, of course, theologize and intellectualize why such evil acts happen in our world. Yet, the questions I believe we also need to struggle with are those that lead us to a place of hope in the midst of a sad and disheartening fall. The great poet Emily Dickinson wrote, "Hope is the thing with feathers that perches in the soul, and sings the tune without the words, and never stops at all…" Maybe the questions that we have in our hearts and minds come from that place of hope that is the very essence of our souls. Autumn, even one as difficult as this, can raise the questions about what really matters—where do you place your hope?

There will always be autumnal times in your life, even if not as pronounced as those of today. The fall dramatically reminds us that the only constant is God, and God calls all of humanity to a vision beyond that of hurtful behavior, hate and violence. It is a vision that raises questions of how you may serve so that evil does not win out and we move closer to where all people may live peacefully with one another. These are questions that are worth, and indeed demand, all of your attention.

The autumn is here and questions will continue to emerge in these changing times. Yet God will remain constant. And it is here where you may place your hope and focus upon the questions of what unites us and how we may serve one another. The leaves will continue to fall but your spirit can rise and lead you to a better place—a place of service and hope.

THANKFULNESS IN A TIME OF WAR

The images of my Thanksgivings past are focused upon the sights and smells of our home as the turkey dinner-feast was being prepared. If I close my eyes, I can almost smell the turkey dinner in the oven and see the frost that formed upon the kitchen windows on those cold Long Island Thanksgivings. These are images that mirror in some respects the artistic work of Norman Rockwell in his familiar painting of a family's joyful turkey dinner called, *Freedom from Want.*

This painting was one in a series of four entitled: *The Four Freedoms: Freedom from Want, Freedom from Fear, Freedom to Worship,* and *Freedom of Speech.* They were Rockwell's contribution to the war effort and were birthed in Franklin Delano Roosevelt's 1941 *State of the Union Address.* In the painting, *Freedom from Want,* the artist captures around the dinner table a great picture of thankfulness in a time of war.

Sixty years later we find ourselves in a time that mirrors in many ways those Thanksgivings of the past. Our unique images of Thanksgiving are once again interwoven with images of war—images that are all at once horrific, sad, heroic and spirited. Perhaps this season, a time of commemorating the pilgrim colonists' feast of 1621, gives rise more than usual to my deep heartfelt emotions that beg the question, "For what am I thankful?"

Growing up I heard stories from my father of World War II, when he was just a young boy in a family that struggled to make ends meet. One day that struggle was made even harder, as his family heard the news that his oldest brother had been killed in a tank battle halfway around the world. I wonder if their Thanksgiving seemed different that year—if thankfulness was difficult or perhaps more pronounced? I wonder today whether Thanksgiving in America is different—different for those who lost loved ones on September 11th, different for all of us as we pause to reflect around the dinner table.

I believe that throughout America there will again be a great picture of thankfulness in a time of war. Will you be thankful for the same four freedoms that Americans were thankful for when Norman Rockwell painted them? Will you be thankful for those that work to uphold and defend these freedoms? Will you be thankful for a nation with enormous opportunities and resources? Maybe this thankfulness will today more powerfully remind you of the divine call to share those blessings with those in need, so that freedom from want may one day be true for all.

Thanksgiving is not as much a day as it is an act of giving thanks—an expression of gratitude that is especially directed toward God. I sense that when we pull our chairs up to the table on Thanksgiving Day, we will have also pulled ourselves closer to living in a profound spirit of thanks that is quite different today than before.

SEARCHING FOR PEACE

Recently, as I was driving from one part of our state to another, a song came on the radio that brought me back to my childhood. The words sang out, "Let there be peace on earth and let it begin with me. Let there be peace on earth, the peace that was meant to be." This was the final communion hymn that was sung every week in the little Episcopal Church on Long Island where I first pursued my call to ministry. Yet, reminded in the car at that moment of my response to God's call, I felt that maybe there was another call that I had ignored—maybe it is a call that most of us continue to believe is not really possible in this life. Can peace begin with me?

Each day I awaken to the possibility that the news will be of war, not of peace. Each day I fear the reports of another terrorist attack somewhere in the world; and, I am especially frightened since 9-11 that it could again be on American soil. Today, I hear of United Nations' inspectors in Iraq seeking the presence or evidence of weapons of mass destruction, and I question deep down if peace between America and Iraq is really being sought? We live with the great challenge of desiring a world where peace for our children is possible, and figuring out the means to achieve that goal peacefully. We are confronted with the disturbing paradox of going to war to have peace. I struggle with the question of whether I believe peace is really possible in this world and life?

Perhaps this can be a season of searching for peace. Maybe in this season of preparation to celebrate Christmas, I can focus anew on what this time is really all about—the promise of the peace of Jesus Christ brought into the history of the world more than 2000 years ago. "Peace on earth and mercy mild, God and sinners reconciled," are words that ring out throughout this time, but are they simply a hollow reminder of what we do not believe we will ever experience?

The question for you to consider, especially in this season that celebrates the birth of the Prince of Peace, is whether you are willing to continue to search for ways to peace. Nationally, we must hold our President, Congress and U.S. policies to an accountability that always seeks peace first, before making a decision for war. War at times may be inevitable, but all paths to peace must first be heavily tread upon. The war on terrorism must be understood within the parameters of how it shall eventually bring us peace.

Perhaps in the final analysis the words of the hymn, *Let there be Peace on Earth,* point to the truth that peace is only possible when each of as individuals are in its pursuit. Peace begins with your searching for ways to bring God's peace into the daily activities of your life. Peace is only possible in the broadest context, the world, when we pursue it in the smallest context, one to another. Imagine the possibilities for your life if each of you made this a season of searching for peace, celebrating the promise of peace that little infant brought into the world, and working to make it a reality. May this be a season you say and live the words, "Let peace begin with me." And may you never stop searching for peace.

THE ASHES OF WAR

Ash Wednesday marks the beginning of Lent, one of the holiest seasons in the church year. This is a time in the life of all Christians when we are called to self-examination and repentance. Perhaps the most powerful words of that day are said as the ashes of the earth are crossed upon our foreheads: "Remember that you are dust, and to dust you shall return." This year as I touched those ashes, I still saw the ashes and felt the sadness of September 11th.Yet now there was a new heaviness in my heart for the ashes yet to be created through a possible war with Iraq.

So many of us have spent a great deal of time examining the issues surrounding the United States' and the United Nations' relationship with Iraq, UN resolutions, disarmament, terrorism, etc., and what has brought us to this critical moment in the history of the world. The issues are enormously complex—more complicated and hidden than even the most astute student of foreign policy could completely comprehend. Most likely, there are circumstances known to the intelligence community, of which the average person is completely unaware. The full ramifications of war with Iraq are unknown. What seems to be known is that many in our military, the coalitions, and in Iraq's will perish. Civilians, too, will be wounded and killed, and a civilization will be brought to ashes.

As complicated as the issues are, though, perhaps it is still easier for us to focus upon all of the arguments pro and con for this war—keeping the conversation there offers a sense of comfort and manageability, albeit a false one. However, I believe the greater area of focus for Christians is self-examination and repentance. For in the final analysis there is no other starting point. This is the very place from which the Christian faith originates.

Throughout the worldwide church it is no coincidence that the Lenten season began with the Gospel story of Christ's baptism and subsequent retreat in the wilderness for forty days. This was a period of temptation and self-examination—this wilderness was where Christ lived before he began his ministry and work. And this wilderness place of self-examination and repentance is where I must go as I struggle to make sense of the crisis with Iraq.

As a priest of the church, self-examination and repentance force me to live in an uncomfortable place of tension. I know that the world would be a more secure place without the tyranny of Saddam Hussein. September 11th was a tragic reminder of the real presence and activity of evil in the world. However, it is that very wilderness place of self-examination and repentance that calls you to proclaim that you can never give up on peace. How can you with all that is at stake?

I believe that self-examination brings us to the realization that all of us fall short of God's vision for humanity, and that compels us to want to sit at the table with those from whom we differ and maybe even greatly mistrust. It is true that a military action may prevent a possible future attack, may remove an evil leader, but at what cost? Can we bomb a nation and people into peace, or as some have suggested into a democratic form of government? There are no easy answers, but our faith demands that we sit at the table and exhaust every possibility for peace. And your faith demands that you pray daily for the peace of the world—the hope that God holds out to us when we look beyond the ashes of war.

LIVING IN GOD

Reflections beyond

TRUSTING

Once again I found myself at the beach for a brief retreat. On one of the days it rained; I actually enjoy a day of rain at the beach. I found myself walking the beach late that afternoon and reflecting on a rather serious question: *Why do I trust God?* I don't know what prompted this question—God, perhaps—but there it was for me to grapple with.

It was now *Ordinary Time*, the liturgical season of the church that follows the feast of Pentecost. Paradoxically, *Ordinary Time* begins almost parallel with summertime, which for most of us serves as a break with the ordinary routine of our lives—life slows down a bit. Yet, in both the ordinary and unordinary times of our lives, we inevitably confront the question of our trust in God.

I recall the story of Jairus falling at Jesus' feet and begging for his daughter's life. Christ responds, "Do not fear, only believe." (Mark 5:36) I hear this passage and it is mysterious to me, even jarring. It seems to say something about trusting in God and God's timing. There is great mystery surrounding the practice of trusting in God. Trust in God also seems to be about both God's timing and our own.

Trusting in God is accepting the mystery of that relationship; it is putting our lives fully in God's hands and believing that God will direct us and bring us into fullness. God will be God. And this is easier to accept, of course, when things in our lives are going well—when the prayers seem answered. But what about the difficult and even tragic times of our lives—how are we to trust God then?

What are we to do when we feel attacked on all sides? As a child, I swam in the waters off the coast of Long Island. Often the waves would be crashing in so fast and hard that I would be knocked off my feet several times as I attempted to enter the ocean to swim. What about the difficult and anxious waves of life that literally knock us off our feet as well? Look to the one who walks on water and says, "Quiet, be still." (Mark: 4:39) Keep focused upon Jesus Christ, and trust that he will hear your prayer and bring peace to your heart. Fall at his feet and say, "Lord, have mercy," over and over again.

Within the difficult and tragic times of your life, you must, as Jairus did, look to Jesus, know that God did not cause these times, and look to Jesus again. You must trust that God is with you in your suffering, for that is the promise of the cross of Jesus Christ. You must trust that God's love and grace will ultimately win out because of that cross. And until you are able to fully trust this in your heart, maybe all you can do is fall on your knees and say, "Lord, have mercy."

THE PATH THROUGH WORRY

During the height of the Cold War at the World's Fair, the Russians, at their exhibit, tried to powerfully emphasize the point that peace was possible between the United States and the Soviet Union. It seems they had a cage in which they kept together a lion and a lamb to prove that the lion and lamb really could lie down together. As people toured that exhibit they were absolutely amazed. Finally after several days, someone asked the keeper how it was done. The keeper responded, "Oh it's very simple. We change the lamb every morning."

Like imagining the lion and lamb lying down together peacefully, it is also hard for us to imagine our lives without worry—without anxiety. Yet, St. Paul, in writing to the church in Philippi, proclaims, "The Lord is near. Do not worry about anything, but in everything by prayer and supplication with thanksgiving let your requests be made known to God. And the peace of God, which surpasses all understanding, will guard your hearts and your minds in Christ Jesus." (Philippians 4: 5-7) Could Paul's instruction to the early church really be not to worry? Certainly the early Christians had a great deal of which to be anxious. How can I be without worry?

When I walk past the periodicals at the bookstore and see cover stories on terrorist cell groups, the possibility of biological warfare, a suicide bomber at an outdoor café in Jerusalem, the difficulty of winning the peace in the Middle East, sexual abuse of children by priests, and people in desperate need of work, how am I not to worry? How can I not be anxious? What are the daily things that I worry about? Can I really be someone who does not worry?

I do not believe it is possible not to worry—it is part of the human mind and condition, but there is a path to live through it. Before Paul calls upon the Christians not to worry, he states that God is near, "The Lord is near." Turn over everything to God in prayer with thanksgiving. The path through our worries is to practice the presence of God in our lives. Paul goes on to say that we should think about those things that are true, those things that are honorable, those things that are just, whatever is pure, whatever is pleasing, commendable—whatever is excellent. Maybe I should look for incidental sacraments, the outward beauty and activity of God that is around us everyday in the ordinary. The path through worry may be found in our focusing upon these incidental sacraments, if you will, and through them experiencing God's grace. Do you practice this kind of presence of God in your life?

You cannot stop worrying by simply practicing mind over matter. The path through worry is through the practice of seeing God's presence in your life, in all situations, and at all times. This is what leads to God's peace in your life—a peace that will always surpass my ability to understand the things you actually worry about and go through. It is a peace that ultimately will keep your heart and mind in Christ Jesus. It is that peace that empowers you to proclaim with Paul, *I can do all things through him who strengthens me.*

HAND OVER HAND

Not so long ago I had the occasion to do the final preparation of two young adults for their baptism into the church and the greater kingdom of God. We spent the better part of the first half-hour rehearsing the choreography of the baptismal service. However, it was in the second unrehearsed half-hour that I experienced transcendence beyond the realm of everyday life, as we touched that kingdom that we proclaim.

We stood at the steps to the chancel that leads to the altar, when she asked, "This may be a stupid question…I am sorry…but, I don't know how I am supposed to receive communion…the bread? I can receive communion after I am baptized can't I?" My response was, "Of course you can. What a great day this will be! You simply place your right hand over your left—hand over hand." And at that moment, I felt that the three of us had mysteriously broken through the confines of Prayer Book rubrics to touch the kingdom of God. Her question, a simple one, pushed us pass the common ritual to the uncommon place of the profound answers we all seek in our faith.

As I prepared these young adults for baptism, I realized that I had not given any thought to their receiving the sacrament of the bread and wine. Yes, this would be their first time to take Jesus Christ into their very beings through Holy Communion. How could I miss that? This young woman's question pointed to a privilege that I can barely remember not having—the privilege of holding out hand over hand before God's holy altar. How many of us take this simple, yet profound, action for granted?

Perhaps a way to examine this question is to look at what we lose when we choose not to place our hand over hand on a regular basis. Christ has promised us that when we bless, break, take and eat bread together that he will be present to us in a way unparalleled by all others. Somehow through the gracious activity of God working through the ministry of the church, the real presence of Jesus is found in the blessed bread and wine. So that when we place hand over hand for the bread, we are literally holding out our hands to Christ's body inviting him into our own. We take Christ's body into our very hearts, bodies, minds and souls, so that we might carry Christ into our worlds of daily existence.

It seems to me that we lose a lot when we keep our hands from God. Of course, there are lots of other ways that our hands are kept busy in this hectic life. But that's just the point isn't it? Do you really want to be in the world of your existence without the power of Christ's full presence within you? When you choose to do it on your own, you limit Christ's working through you—you limit God's possibilities for your life when you don't regularly hold out hand over hand, inviting Christ's body into your own.

WORN TILES

There I stood, staring down at the very spot where the shrine of Thomas a' Becket, Archbishop of Canterbury, had once been. The site of the shrine is in Trinity Chapel, near the high altar of England's Canterbury Cathedral. Henry VIII had torn down the shrine in 1538 in an attempt to destroy the monasteries and the power of the church over the state. Yet, by that time the beautiful stone tiles that date back to the 12th century had already been worn down by the thousands of pilgrims that journeyed to Canterbury to pay homage to this saint and worship their Lord. I could not help but notice how these tiles were actually lower than those in other areas of the cathedral, worn by the feet of the faithful.

Many had journeyed to Canterbury following the slaying of the Archbishop. On a cold December night in 1170, as Becket prayed in the northwest transept of the cathedral, with sword in hand four of Henry II's knights put him to death. Chaucer's Canterbury Tales tells of a knight, solicitor, nun, squire, parson, merchant, miller and others on their way in pilgrimage to the site of this martyrdom. And it is so amazing that those pilgrimages continue to Canterbury Cathedral today; the tiles are still being worn down by the faithful.

There was something profoundly revealing in considering those worn tiles. Could it not be said that within our daily lives as Christians there are *tiles* that we wear down—the paths that we continue to choose? If I were able to stare upon the tiles that I have worn down, would I be comforted by the places to which they have brought me? What are my shrines? Where are the worn tiles in my life?

The spiritual journey is at one level a challenge to wear down the tiles that many others would never choose to walk upon. We are called by Christ to walk upon tiles of love, non-judgment, peace, generosity and faithfulness. The life that Jesus Christ has called you to is one that also challenges you to examine the worn tiles that lead you away from God. Where are those places that you should no longer walk? Perhaps they are tiles of prejudice, judgment, anger, selfishness and unfaithfulness?

What are the tiles that you are wearing down? Do they all lead to a deeper living in God? What would your life be like if that were true? You see those are the kind of worn tiles for which God yearns.

SACRIFICE

We were just weeks into the American led world effort to end terrorism and there were numerous rumblings as to when this will all be over. We are a people and a nation that has for some time sought immediate gratification and results—we will have neither in this military, humanitarian and political endeavor. Perhaps, though, our faith lives reveal the posture that we must firmly assume.

At the heart of the Christian faith, and indeed a centerpiece of most of the world's great religions, we find a theology of sacrifice. Sacrifice is defined as, *forfeiture of something highly valued for the sake of something considered having a greater value or claim.* For Christians, of course, the ultimate sacrifice is that of God's Son, Jesus Christ. The greatest Christian symbol is that of the cross—a symbol of sacrifice. But are we in this post-modern world willing to seriously engage the notion and challenge of sacrifice? Are members of a faith, or simply good people, willing to embrace sacrifice as it applies to their daily lives?

When was the last time that you were asked to make a sacrifice? How do you even hear that word? Recently I heard the word sacrifice on national television, but in terms of baseball. The World Series saw both the Yankees and the Diamondbacks trying to hit a sacrifice fly to score the runner from third. Yet what about your giving something up for a greater good? When was the last time you were asked to respond to such a noble challenge?

Fifty plus years ago, there was a generation of Americans of all ages that were called upon to sacrifice after the terrible 1941 attack upon our nation. History has now repeated itself in 2001—with one exception…this attack was even worse. And the reality is that there are many who are now sacrificing a great deal, in many cases their very lives to defend freedom.

The question before you today is, "What is it that lays claims upon your life for which you are willing to sacrifice?" Could it be freedom and peace? Could it be a safe world for our children where democracy, diversity, religious tolerance and service to those in need are woven tightly into the fabric of humanity? Are you willing to make sacrifices in your daily life for this greater good? It seems to sacrifice is to touch the Divine.

THE NARROW DOOR

There was a time in my ministry when I traveled with several others from Atlanta to Ecuador for the purpose of establishing a companion church relationship. Our trip began in the capital city of Quito, where we met with the Bishop of Ecuador. Together we then began to travel throughout the country, which brought us to some of the most remote and poverty-stricken places that I have ever witnessed.

This journey to Ecuador was one that dramatically altered my relationship with God, and the ministry and life that I would strive to lead. It was not only the incredible poverty that I witnessed that changed me; it was also the fact that I came very close to losing my life. We had been traveling for several hours through a very remote part of the Ecuadorian countryside when I became gravely ill from food poisoning. However, through God's grace, my colleagues were able to locate a medical clinic in the small city that we were approaching. All I remember was being carried through a narrow door and the doctor telling me it was a very close call.

So many have experienced these kinds of life changing events first-hand. 9-11 was such an event for us all. I have witnessed how tragedy and sadness strikes our lives and the lives of others—at times, it is very difficult to understand life and the spiritual journey. Yet, God is forever with us and calling us to a life that invites us to be all that we can be in our work, our play, our relationships and most importantly for God. Jesus taught his followers to, "Strive to enter through the narrow door." (Luke 13:24) Jesus proclaimed that we had the ability to choose a different way—the world will always seek to enter through the big and comfortable doors, yet we can choose the narrow one for God.

To choose *the narrow door* means that your life will be different, for you will always make choices based upon your relationship with God through Jesus Christ. And this means every part of your life will be affected—for the narrow door is to live and give your life for Christ. So have you chosen the narrow door? Do you strive always to enter through this door of God's offering—a door that is narrower, much narrower, than that of the worlds'?

THE DRIVE HOME

We listened to *Hootie and the Blowfish, The Beatles,* and *Faith Hill.* We listened to each other reminisce about funny stories and good times of the summer days just past. We listened to the tiredness and even the sadness in each other's voices. We listened to the silence in the car—we were driving home.

Earlier that afternoon a melancholic feeling came over me as I walked up from the beach for the last time and prepared to gaze out at the ocean and listen to the surf just one more time. It was the kind of sadness that masks a deep happiness and joy from the experience of a wonderful time now coming to an end. I was deeply grateful for this vacation of rest and renewal with my family, and now it was time to drive home.

The drive home from the beach, the mountains, or wherever, is a poignant reminder that home is the place to which we must always return. Home is the place that calls out to us wherever we find ourselves. Home is the place that we really never fully leave behind. Home is the collective experience of all of our days—the physical places in which we have lived, our relationships, our work and our play. Perhaps though above all else, home is living in the knowledge of our being at one with the God that dwells within each and every one of us.

To understand living your daily life as being at home with God each day, is to live the life that God hopes for you. The spiritual journey is about your coming to know each day of your life, wherever you find yourself either physically or emotionally, as always being at home with God. Another way of understanding this is to come to the realization that wherever you go, there you are, and there God is, as well. And it is often the home within the community of the church that provides the foundation from which our faith is able to build and grow.

Every once in while, the spiritual journey comes together in such a way that we feel fully at home with God and ourselves. I was on my way home—the drive home—when just such a thing happened to me. Suddenly the melancholy and the sadness of a vacation coming to an end was overtaken by an understanding that the spiritual life and journey is about always being at home with God. This is what God hopes for you—to always be at home in this way.

LOVE NEVER FAILS

I was once again preparing to write in my journal—a particular discipline of my spiritual life—and had a clear subject in mind that I was seeking to address. As I looked up from the screen of my laptop that subject matter no longer seemed relevant. Instead, I watched a couple well into the late years of their earthly life show great affection for one another as they sat holding hands and sipping coffee.

One of the cafes in which I enjoy spending time—coffee in one hand and the laptop in the other—is also a regular place of visitation for a group of senior adults from a local assisted-living facility. This day one particular couple within that group caught my attention not once, but twice, as I sensed from across the room a love that they had for one another that had not failed them, even as so much of their physical health apparently had. The interchanges between them were a poignant reminder of the possibility of a love that never fails in a life that seems often to be filled with failed loves and unloving acts.

Seeing this couple's love proclaimed silently, yet strongly, the words of St. Paul in his First Letter to the Corinthians: "Love is patient, love is kind. It does not envy, it does not boast, it is not proud. It is not rude, it is not self-seeking, it is not easily angered, and it keeps no record of wrongs. Love does not delight in evil but rejoices with the truth. It always protects, always trusts, always hopes, and always perseveres. Love never fails." (1 Corinthians 13:4-8a) St. Paul, I remembered, was speaking to a church filled with new Christians grappling with how to simply get along in their new life in Jesus Christ. So Paul proclaims to them what the love of God holds out to all who aspire to live their lives within that faith and promise. This is, of course, why we hear this passage read over and over again within the context of the celebration of holy matrimony. It is what we all desire for the relationship of husband and wife, and indeed for every relationship both personal and professional.

Yet so many times love does seem to fail us. What about that marriage we worked so hard at only to have it come to a difficult end? What about that relationship with a child that, despite constant work and attention, seems to be stagnated? What about that friend whose love now absent we always thought we could count on? What about our loved one whose love was seemingly taken away from us at an all too early age? And what about the events of September 11th, terrorism in Israel, and the wars in Afghanistan and Iraq?

The harsh reality is that human love does at times fail us. However, that failure in no way diminishes the words of Paul that express God's ultimate love. And the spiritual life is one that calls you to a life that seeks to live in this love in every relationship and situation, despite the possibility of human failure—yours, or someone else's. This is an honest love. It is the very love of God that never fails you even when others may. Maybe its like holding hands with God and sipping coffee. Love always hopes, always perseveres—*Love never fails.*

THE SPIRITUAL PACE

Running on a treadmill provides excellent time to think, or if one prefers, to not think at all. On this particular day I was thinking about how I wanted to increase my mileage covered in a specific amount of time—I had to increase my pace. So now I was running at a faster pace covering more miles, but, of course, on a treadmill still not physically getting any further. I laughed to myself about the whole notion of treadmills, and how they mirror many aspects of our lives, even our spiritual lives.

During the holy season of Lent, much of our focus within the church and as individual Christians is on how we might strengthen and deepen our lives in God. Lent is a particularly reflective time when we examine our individual and corporate spiritual journeys as baptized persons called into a particular life in Jesus Christ. As Christians we cannot speak of the spiritual life apart from our relationship to God through Jesus Christ, and yet a large part of our struggle is with what this life should look like? What should my spiritual journey be about?

The tendency during Lent is often an attempt to *pick up the pace* of our spiritual life. In many ways this is helpful. Often we begin by being more faithful to corporate worship—a critical part of the spiritual journey and life. Many take on additional worship and educational offerings as well. Some may even begin a new ministry or service project. In these ways the pace of our faith life quickens, and I believe this is very good.

However, the interesting paradox of the spiritual life is that for your life to deepen in Jesus Christ, for your relationship with God to reach new levels, you must simultaneously *slow down the pace.* You must slow down in ways that enable you to hear the God with whom you desire a closer relationship. The only way that you can accomplish this is to take some time apart for just God and yourself. Maybe you can sit in silent meditation for ten minutes each day. Maybe you can take a silent walk or run early or late in the day. Maybe through a favorite activity you are able to focus only on God.

Running on a treadmill involves both *picking up* and *slowing down* the pace—both are necessary for a good run. So it is with the Christian's spiritual life. Lent is especially a time when we should explore ways to both *pick up* and *slow down* the pace of your spiritual life. In the final analysis, finding a balanced spiritual pace to your life will deepen and strengthen your life in Christ well beyond the forty days of Lent.

LIVING TOWARD A VISION

The fundamental truth that a vision is needed for us to thrive and prosper as a people is as old as the Hebrew and Christian scriptures. Proverbs instructs us that, "Where there is no vision the people perish." (Proverbs 29:18)

Perhaps the uncertainty of our future since the tragic events of September 11th has keenly brought before us the importance of having a clear vision for our lives. Vision begs the question of our individual and corporate lives, *what really matters?* And I believe that the essential components of a vision must include honesty, accountability and a steadfastness of the will.

So what then does it mean to live toward a vision? We must begin as a people by honestly addressing our present situations—the good and the not so good—and then begin to listen to where we are being called. Of course, I believe that God is always at work calling us to all that God would have us be. The problem so often is that we are not listening, and what is worse is that more often than not we are unwilling to assess our present state of affairs with honesty. When we are honest with where we are, then we are empowered to move toward a vision of where we believe we can be.

As we begin to articulate a vision, it becomes ever so important that we have in place a system of accountability. Accountability, accountability, and accountability—as we have watched corporate scandals unfold before our eyes, the lack of proper accountability is stunning. Yet even more than that, maybe it speaks to the natural desire of humanity to prefer to not be accountable to anyone. This, too, is as old as the genesis of time when God asks in the garden of first humanity, "What have you done?" When you decide that you are going to live toward a vision, then you must also enumerate those ways that you will be accountable to others, yourself, and, ultimately, God.

The famous college football coach, Lou Holtz, once said, "If you don't make a total commitment to whatever you're doing, then you start looking to bail out the first time the boat starts leaking. It's tough enough getting that boat to shore with everybody rowing, let alone when a guy stands up and starts putting his life jacket on." To live toward the vision of where you are being called by God requires a steadfastness of your will. There will always be circumstances and people that attempt to dissuade you. However, it is through perseverance toward that vision that you will draw ever closer to your destination. A vision is always centered upon what really matters, is discovered when you are honest, and is carried out through accountability and steadfastness. Vision is what keeps you moving forward as a person; it is what keeps you from perishing…the way that God calls you to new life.

WHAT REALLY MATTERS

Seven funerals within a week-and-a-half have given rise to this reflection. It seems to be all too easy for us to quickly lose perspective in life on ***what really matters***—illness and death seem to awaken this perspective.

What really matters in life is not your position, but that you are working at what you really love.

What really matters in life is not the good opinion of others about you, but what you and God know in your heart to be true about yourself.

What really matters in life is not the amount of material wealth you have accumulated, but what percentage of that wealth you have given back to God.

What really matters in life is not how good you are at what you do, but that you are striving to do your very best.

What really matters in life is not how much you say, but how well you listen.

What really matters in life are not how many people understand you, but how many people you have worked to understand.

What really matters in life is not our differences, but the ground that we have in common.

What really matters in life is not competing with others, but competing with yourself to be all that God has called you to be.

What really matters in life is not what you say, but that you act with truthfulness and integrity.

What really matters in life is not what we say about our worship of God, but that we show up to worship God.

What really matters in life is not that you have given your children everything that they have asked for, but that you strive to model everything that they should be.

What really matters most in life is your relationship to God through our Lord Jesus Christ.

FINDING GROUND ZERO

I had not been back to the city in which I once lived since that fateful day of September 11th. This was an intentional trip, perhaps even better understood as a pilgrimage, to the site of ground zero. As I got into that New York City cab at 49th and Park on a beautiful summer day of 2003, I asked the driver to bring me to ground zero. He hesitated and looked back at me and said, "How would you like to go?" I responded, "I'm sure you know the best way." With now even more hesitation in his voice, the cabbie confessed, "This is only my second day on the job, I really don't know how to find ground zero." And so my journey began.

As we came up Wall Street heading south, I looked up to my right and did not recognize the city sky, for its emptiness was both foreign and melancholic. As a lump began to form in my throat, I asked the driver to drop me off. I paid and thanked him, and continued to stare at the enormous and unrecognizable hole in the sky. I walked two short blocks and stood at ground zero.

Nothing could have prepared me for what was to follow. If it were not for all of the people and the fear of embarrassment, I would have fallen to my knees in grief. There is a great transparent fence that surrounds the site of the former World Trade Towers. Across the top of the fence, the names of those who gave their lives that day are inscribed—they seem to go on forever. I found my place next to a red rose that had been wedged in the links of the fence, and I gazed out upon the vast emptiness, where less than two years earlier great buildings filled with God's people had stood. And I began to sob uncontrollably.

There is an overwhelming feeling of grief in that place. Today the blocks are all cleaned up, so that if you did not know better it would seem to be a large construction site. Oh but we do know better; we know of the more than two thousand lives lost on that ground. The dirt of the ground holds the ashes of their lives, and the air that is breathed holds the spirits of their lives. It is so very sad. But just as I was feeling self-conscious of my tears, I looked again this time to my right. And there with power and grace stood the natural cross of steel that had been found in the midst of the devastation. The cross was permanently anchored in that ground marking the place as hallowed, where because of a horrific act, so many came to see God face to face. Yet, that cross even more poignantly stands as a symbol of resurrection and hope not only for the lives lost, but also for a world that seeks a way to live together today.

Now two years later, our nation has been involved in three major wars: the war on terrorism, war with Afghanistan, and the war with Iraq. All three are intrinsically linked one to another, and all have taken the lives of more men and women of many nations, tongues and religions. Peace has still not been found...the jury is still out on whether or not we are safer today than yesterday. Certainly that is our prayer.

As I stood at ground zero, two years later, I saw an image from God of a great table in that vast open space. This was a table that God had set, where all people—Christian, Muslim, Jew and all faiths; American, Arab, European, Asian and every nationality; all of God's children, were sitting together and seeking a way forward to not only survive, but fully live. The table of mutual respect, understanding, consensus, charity and peace where all are invited and have a place is our only choice, if we are to ever avoid another 9-11.

Certainly some, like the terrorists, will not ever come to the table. However, the rest of us must lead by example and take our rightful places. We must get out of the mindset of winners and losers. Leadership is about finding the "win-win." That is my dream. That is my hope. Whatever shape ground zero eventually takes as a memorial and new place of business, we will have only really found ground zero, when we have as well found that table for all of God's people.

Epilogue

IT IS NEVER FINISHED

"A jar full of sour wine was standing there. So they put a sponge full of the wine on a branch of hyssop and held it to his mouth. When Jesus received the wine, he said, 'It is finished.' Then he bowed his head and gave up his spirit." (John 19:29-30) And so I imagine Jesus the Christ in the last moments of his life, as his body, mind and spirit hung heavy and in great agony on the hard wood of the cross—finished.

At times I fantasize about what it would presently be like at the end of each workday to *clock out.* During my seventeenth and eighteenth years of life, I worked part-time at a medical center. I was a part of the team that worked to get the meals out in a good and timely fashion to the patients of that large New York hospital. Each day there were two eight-hour shifts—six to two, or two to ten. As you went down into the kitchen, you would first stop in front of an enormous black clock hanging on the wall. Here I would search for my name on a card that hung in a rack adjacent to the clock, it was my time card, push it into the slot of the clock and hear that punch—you have begun.

What has stayed with me about that experience all of these years later is the image of the employees watching the clock. As the close of the shift approached, the workers, no matter where they found themselves, began to wind down and wait to head for that big black clock. Push that card into the slot of the clock and hear that punch—it is finished.

The work and ministry of my life at the cathedral is such that it is never finished. I never shut down my computer and turn off the lights in my office and say, "it is finished." I suppose that is more often true than not for most people. There are common experiences in life that never feel, or in reality are, finished. When raising children, we know that we are never really finished in that parenting role, especially the worrying aspect. No matter what age we find ourselves, if we have taken that responsibility seriously, we continue to the very end trying to guide our children along the right path and worrying all the way. I also remember an experienced and wise artist once saying to me, "At some point you just have to lay the brush down and decide that the painting is finished." I remember asking her, "but how do you know when that is?" She responded, "you just lay the brush down otherwise it is never finished."

Jesus had carried that heavy cross all the way to Golgotha—*the place of the skull.* I suspect that he probably collapsed onto the cross before they nailed him to it. As they lifted that cross up, the weight of his beaten body must have slumped toward the earth. I would imagine, as well, that he came in and out of consciousness before his death—and it was at those moments of clarity that he spoke his words from the cross. Can I ever internalize the experience and extent of his suffering on the cross? Can I ever fully understand that it was for me? And how was it that Jesus knew it was finished?

At the time that Jesus was baptized by John in the Jordan, God spoke from the heavens to declare to those gathered and to the world that he was the Son of God, with whom he was very pleased. This was the true beginning of Christ's journey—his mission and ministry of teaching, healing, forgiving and proclaiming the kingdom. That journey would, of course, ultimately lead to his suffering and death on the cross. "It is finished." Then he bowed his head and gave up his spirit.

Jesus, as God's Son, knew that he had reached that most profound moment in the history of the world, when all human suffering for all time would be incorporated into this one act by God on the cross. Jesus could utter those words because he brought his journey to the place where forevermore all human suffering, violence, war, oppression, shame, guilt, loneliness and hunger, would be also the experience of God. Humanity could no longer be alone in its sufferings because God, in and through Jesus, had suffered it all and would continue in this relationship with us forever. The journey of Christ brought him to that cross, and there it was forever *finished.*

The spiritual journey is always about your living more and more into the life to which you are called by God. This is a life that is made possible because Jesus did finish his journey through his suffering death on the cross. Through that incredible sacrifice the possibility for all of humanity to have a close and purpose-filled life with God was realized.

I have to admit that at times I find it very frustrating being on a journey that never feels finished. In fact, so many areas of my life are not finished. Certainly your spiritual journey is not finished, but maybe in that acceptance you can find comfort and joy. You can be drawn to the cross because it is the very symbol of a finished journey calling you to continue on yours. On the night before his death, Jesus said to his disciples: "A little while, and you will no longer see me, and again a little while, and you will see me…Very truly, I tell you, you will weep and mourn, but the world will rejoice; you will have pain, but your pain will turn into joy...So you have pain now; but I will see you again, and your hearts will rejoice, and no one will take your joy from you...Ask and you will receive, so that your joy may be complete." (John 16:16, 20, 22, 24)

These are difficult and sad days of terrorism and war in which we find ourselves living. Yet they are also days that through God's grace, powerfully remind you of the unfinished nature of the Christian spiritual life. Christ was able to proclaim from the cross, "It is finished," because it was. You must say, "It is never finished," because it never is. These are days that challenge you now more than ever to live and use your life for the greater purposes of God—a God who has not changed since 9-11.

0-595-30413-3